LESSONS
OF LIFE

LESSONS OF LIFE

Evan W. Jones

authorHOUSE®

AuthorHouse™ LLC
1663 Liberty Drive
Bloomington, IN 47403
www.authorhouse.com
Phone: 1-800-839-8640

Published by AuthorHouse   11/04/2013

ISBN: 978-1-4918-3174-8 (sc)
ISBN: 978-1-4918-3173-1 (e)

Library of Congress Control Number: 2013919994

Any people depicted in stock imagery provided by Thinkstock are models,
and such images are being used for illustrative purposes only.
Certain stock imagery © Thinkstock.

This book is printed on acid-free paper.

Because of the dynamic nature of the Internet, any web addresses or
links contained in this book may have changed since publication and may
no longer be valid. The views expressed in this work are solely those of
the author and do not necessarily reflect the views of the publisher, and
the publisher hereby disclaims any responsibility for them.

The Warrior

A life of solitude
Training for that day
Being the best of the best
With minor flaws
Living without fear
And fearing not even death,
Knowing death will come,
In time we will prevail without
Due caution,
Mist of battle our soul will raise victorious,
Knowing this life of solitude is meant for the free

I open

These eyes grow weak,
Strain to see thy door,
Trickle of light, dust filters in,
I open
Thy foot walks cautious,
To feel light warmth thee life,
I open
Thy chains rustic,
Smelt of freedom
Wounds of captivity
Sour thy light
I open
Reaching, knees weak
Prayers answered
Hunger thy breathe,
Finally, we are not forgotten
To some have been
POW/MIA

Live or Die

Live to the fullest
Standing on the edge
Never to second guess my enemy
Train for extremes
Living that day,
By countless moments
Walking deaths rail,
Live or die
Example to live by
Knowing one self, better for
Enemies to guess
Train your mind, never give up
Live to the fullest,
Smile at deaths door.

Damn Few

They are elite
Hardest trials to become one,
They give all
Small fighting force
Covering the globe,
Frogmen they are called
Warriors of the sea
Code of honor
Humble they may be
The damn few
Code of ethics they live
Brother for brother
They are the best of the best
Damn few

Darkness

We sit here waiting
Staring into darkness
Waiting for the sound
Sky lights as 4th of July
Focusing on shadows,
Target,
Running for cover
Shot rings out
He falls,
Darkness
We sit here waiting.

Mile

I walk the miles,
Seen shore lines
Experiences of gold
Smelt death in many ways
Held many dying breaths
Looked upon countless reminders
Scars and tatts' remind why,
I had to do it
Take the souls of others
By these hands
What reminds
I breathe the air as I take your last
I walk the miles, though you can't

I pray

Close my eyes
Pray thy lord my soul
Sounds of battle rage
Escape my vast,
Nightmares begin of terror
Night engulf of sweat
Grasps the air,
Fallen to unmark grave
Thom of hero's
Never return
Pray thy lord, take away
Pain a waits,
I awake in hell.

Welcome Home

The bagpipes play
A flag draped
Twelve men stand lean,
As people stand in line,
That never knew the brave soul
A hero, home finally
Ashes to ashes, dust to dust
Tears of sorrow
This brave man fell
Shots ring out, taps played
His pain rested
Children salute, as his coffin passes
Welcome home son
Stand at ease

Homeless

Weather is cold and harsh
I pull this holey blanket near,
Eat my last can of food
My clothes smell of 30 day stench,
This bottle is dry
40 gallon burns off in the night,
I sleep with one eye open
To watch thieves of the night,
I wonder if I still awake.
I once protected this land
Now I beg for a dollar.
To homeless vets

The Battle

Wars are fought throughout time,
The battle never ends there,
For those that know
By scars on the outside,
To the ones that are hidden,
We fought to bleed for freedom
The freedom that has no time for vets
We lose so many to images
That haunts us daily,
Guilt, rage, and the unknown
By this in ones eye fighting with nightmares,
Others will never understand
We fought the wars
For our brothers
Coming home is the beginning for us.

PTSD
Never forget the sacrifice of those who fought for it.

Pray

My knees are worn
Tears have dried
Some answered
Some ignored,
Are they really answered?
Pamphlets handed out
For a higher power,
Pray harder, you will be
Answered they say,
My eyes grow weary
To the ones that do others wrong,
As they are blessed,
I faultier by disappointment
But I still pray,
May we be answered?

Faith

What is faith?
Is it a spirit?
Is it making believe?
Is it what we need to live?
To grow, for energy, to fantasize for
Could it be a metaphor?
Faith is blessed to us,
Believe in higher power,
Strive for life; give life, share life, and death
We lose faith by hope,
Crisis we gain faith
Pull thru harsh times,
What happens, when all are bless?
Faith gain by belief, touched in ways science wonders
It's in each of us,
Believe in more, strive for a goal
Only you and god know in faith.

Greed

In many styles
A sin that most suffer
Wanting more by taring families apart
The sinner with no remorse
Acts as thankful as ones that are,
Turn a cheek when love ones are at a lost
Only by greed, they feel secure
Can't see what they already lost
Until it's too late

Lust

A sin that I suffer
Wanting to taste
Every woman's beauty crosses my path
Only to know the lonely
Wondering times to close thy eyes,
To quince my thirst
Instead of crossing paths,
Lust, many have died for, and others burned for
Ask thee father to forgive
To lust for life, than sin for thirst

Temptation

Lived a life of thirst,
Chasing time of vigilance
Leaning towards temptation
When I see them,
Perfection, skin soft to touch,
Lips of candy,
Eyes to melt to the soul
My mouth dries
Thirsting of a woman,
Temptation of a woman,
Lingers the mind
Only to satisfy what you may have,
To lose what you've already gained
Temptation will kill thy soul

Born

Life is a choice,
With avenues to succeed
Or to lose by choice,
Belief we are all born in sin,
By only to seek forgiveness'
In which with questions,
Given so much,
Gain but a few,
Choices broken promises
Life a blink of an eye,
We so few, endless souls
Search patterns in life
Only gaining what's given to
Promises broken,
Born to life,
We breathe to die
For your life
What to destine for

The World

Has become bitter,
Darkness has prevail more
As good men held
Against their own,
Greed and unselfish acts
Overrun the vast,
Individuals become their own enemy,
Will time last
This vast plain of ignorance,
The world
Bitter sweet sympathy
As darkness prevails
Good of man may rise of the sword

Questions

Do you question reasons of life?
Failing as others do
Believe thy faith has thy sin,
Reasons of life, makes us who we shall
Be
Not who we become
Pound issues in sand,
Splitting the heart of soul,
Question your reasons of failing
Instead climb thy mountain,
Grow with others
Instead of hate
Hold your roots,
Stand in front with those that don't stand alone,
Be the one, take failures
Into positive roles
Your soul burns of desire,
Only the jealous fears

Best Advice

Each day is a gift
Not a given right
Leave no stone unturned
Live without fear
Try to take the path less traveled
Against the grain
Is the way of life
Don't take the free line
Live life as the last day,
Take the chance to
Shot for the stars,
Live life with no regrets
Best advice
Can be the last,
Each day is a gift,
Live your life as the last day

Our Talent

Our gifts
So over looked,
Rather try impress
A lifetime,
Than challenging
Your talents,
Worry what others say,
Than laugh at them,
To climb the highest
Sacrifice we must,
Let go of fears
Talents are here
Challenge what god gives you

Dreams

As children our minds
Drift off in places far known,
We grow to hold
Loosing dreams to be,
Dreams that hurt
Dreams that end
Dreams to live for
Only to move forward
Holding on, second guessing
In the end to accomplish
Is devotion

Flaws

In many times
I set fourth achievement
Greater than others
But flawed by personal mistakes,
Mistakes that which burnt
Soul by mind,
Only to those that have
Looked down upon I,
I've gained respect of hundreds
Than those of a higher power,
By flaws they felt to judge
As I smirk in disgust,
I look to those to follow
As I lead greater accomplishments
Than that of gold,
With flaws, I prevail higher

Police

The streets are harsh
Filled by evil, judgmental people
We look to each other
To battle alone,
Ridicule by others
No matter the circumstances
We take an oath, wear a badge of honor
Give up our lives for strangers
Our families suffer the lost,
Still to be judge by others
A job well done
We look to each other
To battle alone
We are the thin blue line
To be tried by twelve
Or be carried by six,

Police Officer

I strap a belt with a gun everyday
Pray that I don't take a life
I wear a badge of honor
Pray for the shield of god
I wear a uniform crisp to view
Pray others hatred be forgiven
I wear a vest to protect thee
Pray to see my children grow up
I stand to protect and serve
Pray for strength to uphold all
If I perish by end of watch
Pray that I stand abreast with
My brothers and sisters that gave
Ultimate sacrifice by heavens gates,

Blue Line

Our lives are different
Others despise us,
We stand alone
When others fear,
We take an oath
As others break laws,
We walk the streets
While you sleep peacefully,
Our families pray for us
When others pray not to see us,
We are the guardians
Against those who prey on the weak,
We are the blue line
Try us, and see what happens

Veterinarians

Their touch is healing
Unselfish demeanor to help
Voice for the ones that can't voice,
They work endless hours
To save our pets and homeless
Animals,
Their hearts are kind
To heal the wounds
To mend the broken
To save ageing to new science,
They answer calls when
The day ends without hesitation,
To bring satisfaction to
You and I,
Unsung heroes
Gratitude is their devotion
Veterinarians one of gods
Greatest creations

The Race

Speed through the water,
Wind in my face, sun to my back
In chase for a prize
Concentration, skill, determination, and knowledge
Wins the day,
Or just plain luck
The bass run deep
As time is a nail bitter,
The final weigh in
Anxiety flow the competition,
Heads bow-down with smart remarks,
A smile broadens the pack
Big bass is in
It's a game, are you in?

Bass

I watch my line come taught,
A bass to surprise
Joy lingers, to fight a beast,
Only to respect Mother Nature
Watch the mighty swim free,
Another prize I hold
Cast along shorelines
Trolling the depths
Waiting another fight
I search,
Testing time, testing wits', testing skill
Watch my line come taught
A bass to surprise,
Joy lingers to fight such delight
Closest you'll be to god

The Sky

I stood along the drive
Starring to the sky,
Amazement the stars glow as the sun,
Tracing the gods I look upon
As I to be a child again,
Never before a night had I gazed
Upon before,
Captivating I say,
Fireflies dance as beacons of the sea,
I close my eyes
To take the moment in,

The Field

Overgrown by weeds
Memories were made,
Stories still told by friends
The field
Children played, games were won and lost,
To those that look upon this field,
Our children played as heroes, or we may have,
The bases have faded
Dugouts grown over,
The memories are fresh,
Fresh cut grass of game day,
As cheers and laughter fade
With a highway close by,
The field
Cherished memories
Running the bases, one more time

Bass 2

He hunts deep within
Waiting to ambush its prey,
Predator of senses,
Doesn't forgive
Chased by determined anglers,
Witty, beautiful and masterful
A trophy to others,
Bloodline to me
Marvelous to catch, hard to defeat
Keeper within, a hunter to be hunted,

River

A river runs
Smooth rocks, uncover
Hidden secrets of life,
Water flows, never freezes
Never dries, and never dies,
Full of life, breathing tears of heaven
Etching valleys of life
We trace steps of rivers,
Which tell of stories?
Those have yet to be uncovered,
And darkness hides deep within,
My life runs of a river

My sweetheart

I seen her as a young woman
To grow separately thru life,
Always to wonder what we could have been,
Only I be to self with children,
Her to wed with family
Still when paths cross,
We look at each waiting for that
Taste once again,
Only to walk away wondering,
My sweetheart
You are my friend,
I am here for you, as I was in school

Trish

Her flower

Her flower grows,
Blooms of elegance,
Truer than words
Nectar sweet delight,
Sways by the wind,
Her aroma lingers my buds,
Her roots run deep that can't be displaced,
Her flower grows
Blooms of elegance,
Her thorns hidden
Protection only for those who lie,
Her pathway only for one that's truer,
Her flower,
I keep her bloomed

With Hope

So much to know
I wonder your heart,
Smile never felt before,
Sweetness of untold stories,
Guessing new lands of you
Truer than anyone knew,
Given light to a man that closed,
Waited to long for someone like you,
Never knew I could feel this again,
My heart rises for you, as wait for you

If You Could

If I could say
What you may see,
Your hell come my pain,
If you only knew, knowing that scar
Runs deep within,
Never heels this one soul,
A soul you cursed,
With a curse you walked with,
If I could say
What you may see,
Your hell come my pain,

To You

To you lost in life,
Lost by words,
Mentality it devours you,
Fears known, to be unknown
To you
Gaze upon endless shadows,
Lost in space,
Physically dried as ripe prunes,
Mentality vanquished you've become,
To you
Screams ring of bells
Trapped, lost in life of padded walls
In walls, nobody knows of you,
Scream, nobody cares of you,
To you
The life has pushed to the end,

Wait

I a wait for you by candles,
Waiting to lie upon,
To melt silently into your lust,
Candles flicker as our bodies move the sheets,
Temperature rises, while windows fog
Figures locked in place,
Candles burn of delight,
Climax rips the sheets,
I a wait for you by candles
To melt silently, softly into your lust

The temptation

When I see you near,
To run my fingers thru your hair,
Tasting your lips,
Feeling your body burn for mine,
As I look deep in your eyes,
Lost in the moment,
Savoring your taste,
As I undress your hour glass,
My fingers tip toe a long your curves,
Tasting your innocence
As you gasp for air,
The temptations as you walk by,
Only linger in my mind

By Far

I long the distance,
Alone to long
Longing for a chance,
To taste the sweetness
I vast in waste
Wasting time to love,
I long the distance
By far,
Too long to be alone
Wasting in this vast wasteland

Want You

I watch you from a distance,
Imagine running my fingers in your hair,
Wishing to taste your lips
Feel your body press to mine,
Would give up forever to hold you,
Because I know you feel me know,
I don't want to miss you anymore
Watching you from a distance,
I fight the tears of you,
I want you to know,
Who I am
If I could only show you as you pass,

Last Dance

If I could give one more chance
To dance with you,
Holding you, keeping promises that
Were broken,
Only knowing now the dance is
Quieted by far,
The loneliness has broken,
By chances that endure
The solitude of empty heart beats,
If I could give one more chance to
Dance with you,
Only to know I shouldn't be the
One with you,

I Cross

Cross the river
Touch the ground
Kiss the earth
Be bless by god
Sacrifice my love for life,
Feel the freedom, no war
No cries, pain, agony, no fear,
Just peace
Feel the earth
As he touches your heart
Letting go,
As you walk to him,
This new life
Nothing will hurt you again,
As he welcomes you
Is this heaven?

A Picture

I stare at a picture
Look upon you,
Mind wonders, as my fingers
Dream to trace,
Legs I climb
Eyes dreamt upon lust inside you,
Breast I lay upon
Feel your heart flutter,
Taste of lips
Sweetness of honey,
I dreamt upon you
Starring at your picture

Can't you

I see you
Words unspoken,
Heart races to you
Never seen
What a woman can do,
Can't you see
My life upside down
Till you came in,
Your touch
Magnifies my soul,
Kiss to die for
Holding you tight,
Can't remember this feeling
Till you came in,
Can't you see
Race to you
Feel you, taste you,
Spend that last moment
In your eyes, what a feeling

Change

You hear a song
Dances to your heart
Changes your mind of life,
You live harsh reality
Changes your heart,
Death bellows the soul
Changes the process of life,
Your love walks out
Changes your eyes,
Your world upside down
Changes your walk,
Your children grow
Changes your age,
Your friends move on
Changes your character,
Your god forgives you
You are changed forever,

Darkness

Sit silently, darkness my safety
Drugged passes the pain,
Agony ravages my soul
Silently wait,
Darkness of depression sinks in
On sunny days,
I should feel alive but in darkness
I live,
Climbing the walls screams unheard
Wait in cold sweat,
Tearing to my skin
Drugged passes the pain,
Feeling hopeless
I wait,
Leave while my soul looks on

My journey

I walk the beaten path
Cross the lies,
Climb the mountains
Search thee sites of new,
Bring a horizon
To this life,
Better with less
Dramatic scenes,
Take the sites
Living for the day,
Breathing for that one
Feeling the wind among me,
Taste of freedom
My journey begins of new,
I walk the beaten path
Cross the lies,
As others dwindle
My the past rest in peace

Dreaming out loud

To many times I've made the mistakes
Not pushing threw, coming short,
On my knees, warring these bones old
Dreaming that day will be,
Only in moments I see clear
Screaming to my heart's content,
Not letting go what I dream to be
Dreaming out loud
She only knew that I pray to be
Feeling my strength for her,
In so many ways not to see
My dreams to be,
Dreaming out loud
You see our paths ignite the internal flame,

Chance

I write to you,
Hoping to love more
Waiting for a chance
I broke your heart,
A heart that broke a million times over
To last a lifetime with,
Waiting for a chance,
Chance we should take
To take to mend our love,
Time passes
As sand passes from the clock,
I a wait
As seasons pass by,
My love, will never change for you

The Hall

I walk the hall
Memories pass,
Clock is still
Silence falls,
My heart groans for you
Memories pass
This hall is empty,
Silence groans this home,
As my heart groans for you
I walk the hall
Images of you race as ghost
Down this hall,
Memories pass
As emptiness settles in,

Found You

Laying a lone I see you
Grasping the pillow tight,
As though it was me with you
You toss the words of love,
As the night grows darker
Your mind scatters,
Lost you come to be
Found you,
Laying a lone I see you
Hopelessly I watch you,
Pain, you hold within
Grasping tight to your tears
As though it was me,
My spirit is always with you

My Loss

I lost a father, man of his word,
Salt/ pepper hair, a heart of gold,
Love for family, fishing, and the hokies,
Memories of him good or bad,
All are life lessons to learn by,
Hardships to begin, wishing to hear his voice of reason,
To feel his hand on my back for compliments,
Only I wait to see him again,
I lost a father
He faced Satan head on to battle fate for his family,
He provided, he touched others,
My father the greatest,
He looks over us today,
A savor than a spirit,
I lost my father
A man I wish to be more of,
A man I walk in his foot prints,
My father
Who has left his mark in all of us,

Intentions

I wish you could see,
What my intentions that I have,
If you could read my heart,
To promise not to break yours,
If you only knew,
To have dreams for us to be,
You made me feel as a winner with you,
As I ask for forgiveness by broken promises,
What my intentions that I have,
If you could read my heart,
I pray for you to understand,
All my intentions of loving you,
I seldom get things right,
As you feel that I took you for granted,
But that's not the case,
If you could read my heart,
You would see, I had the best intentions
For loving you,
All I ask is for forgiveness,

Natalie

She's a guardian, who stands firm,
Gentle to touch, a heart of gold,
Always on alert for my children,
A bite that makes you think twice,
A man's best friend, dependable, and brave,
Love for her owner,
Unselfish, and characteristic,
When I'm at my lowest,
She picks me up,
Her black and tan coat,
Glistens in the light,
She is my shepherd,
Who I miss dearly of her passing,
                                    10/11

Katie

Short and stumpy,
Stubborn, but lovable,
Quick on her feet,
A child's toy, and cuddled friend,
Cute to squeeze and soft coat,
Gives a bath when you meet her,
Always looking for trouble,
Her white and brown spots
Makes her fun in the snow,
She is a best friend at heart
But more stubborn than a mule,
My little Russell

Her Hazel

Your hazel eyes, and smile of ease,
Your body of glass as fragile you may-be,
Love of greatness
Touch of healing,
You walk among clouds,
As your tenderness brings a man to his knees,
A beauty within, more than you know,
Your body of fragrance weakens as your touch
To me,
Lips of addiction as a piece of candy,
Her hazel of Sarah,

I Gaze

To gaze in all as your smile lingers in my mind,
A voice of reason to break my walls,
May be a feeling that I could feel again,
You walk by, wishing you would touch me,
I gaze upon you,
Your eyes glow of want,
Your skin soft to want of touch,
To feel my lips gently run of your body,
To imagine yours on mine,
I gaze upon you,
Imagining, needing, wanting and wishing for you,
I gaze in all when you walk by,

My Sons

As I write about my sons,
I felt deeply sadden that I may
Never see them grow,
Life has been hell
Nor did I die to be in hell,
Hell found me living,
I've been cursed by unknown reasons,
Superstitions couldn't curse this soul enough
By which the devil has questioned it,
I don't feel of suicide, but dead within,
I lose so much that others have caused,
I suffer their gain by mental weakness,
To stand alone I've come costumed to,
I pray my children will never go through
What their father has been dragged through,

My Children

I look upon my children to give them all that's needed,
Give my embrace when needed, stay firm of discipline,
Stand to protect them, as I wipe their tears,
Hold them when a bad dream presents itself,
Cheer them when they succeed,
Teach them when their wrong, and the values of life,
My children
As they grow, I grow old too,
I leave a legacy
To be men, than children
To hold honor, than to be cowards,
No matter their path of life,
I am proud of my boys,

Toby

He came to us in a blessing,
After great lost of a friend,
He's true as a shepherd lives
A guardian that stands true,
A best friend, loveable as a child,
He's from the old line of shepherds,
Bigger, faster, patient as kids climb him,
His bark is fierce but gentle to be a lap dog,
Ears lay relax instead to a point,
Saddle back lines the body perfect,
Stance firm as well,
Created to perfection,
Couldn't ask for anything more
Other than to my best friend,

Grace

Once the grace is sang,
Do we stand to figure the words?
Or feel the words lift our soul,
In many ways it's played,
Many times tears fill the air,
By this grace is sung,
Sung with many reasons,
To those we say good bye to,
Do you listen to the words or feel
The last note with understanding

Moonlight

I wish to lay with you,
Feel your lips whisper sweetness,
As your fingers dance along my body,
I melt inside you as you moan delight,
Your body glows as the moon shadows you,
Candles flicker of breath,
Our bodies sequence to silent rhythms,
The taste better is sweet of you, as you taste me,
I wish to lay with you
My delight, I hold you as our bodies melt to the moonlight,

I walked in

I walked in for a meal,
Upon me was a woman that I only
Dreamt of in dreams,
Lost in her eyes I drift off,
As she speaks of accent,
I weaken to stutter words,
Lost I felt to be in a trance,
Everything I could believe to be,
Feelings I haven't felt,
As minutes pass, small talk comes
To an end,
Life unfolds from a meal,
To think of her eyes to be lost in,
Tracing her body, running my fingers through
Her hair,
Feeling our lips melt together,
Could our hearts beat together?
To think this could be someone
I walked in for a meal,

The Unknown

In past we were classmates,
An age of the unknown
We looked upon as smiles,
To images throughout the years,
We come to an age
Older but wiser,
A once school boy crush
Becomes a reality,
Chance of dreams
Unknown to the future presents,
Only to see you again
Brings yearbooks to color,
To gaze upon you as that school boy,
Tried to catch your eye
Has now caught your heart,
An age of the unknown
We look upon ourselves
To what dreams are,
Only to stare to the unknown together,

Fire

We never started it but it's evolved,
The world has evolved to live our lives,
As though no tomorrow but to gain less,
By fires that engulfed those around,
We never started it but it's evolved,
With fires spreading,
Others stand by as evil breaths our lives,
We look for it to dissipate as the serpents' rise,
Waiting for good to prevail,
The world has dissipate,
What has happen to us?

To Rise

To this day has grown old,
As I grown weary of this future,
To understand this path set forth,
I come to past,
To lie awake as I,
Look to understanding other than failure,
A beaten path,
Guided by one,
To be weary as I,
Leap without faith
Only to be placed further past,
I leap with faith to rise once more,
As others may see,
To understand this death,